# About The Che

CW00542871

Hello, my name's John Kirkwood, I am a retired chef, from the north east of England, in the UK, and welcome to my third recipe book. I'm a self-taught chef, that has been in the catering trade for over 35 years, since retiring from our family business, I have found a new passion in sharing some of our favourite recipes on YouTube.

You can view most recipes in this book, via video format on YouTube.

@

www.youtube.com/user/jonboy2478

You can view any of my recipes in this book, by scanning the QR codes with your smart device.

# Disclaimer

The reader must take full responsibility for their own safety and hygiene, when replicating any of my recipes in this book. The kitchen can be a dangerous place to work, please be careful. Also be very aware of allergies.

John Kirkwood holds no responsibility for any harm caused while making any of these recipes.

John Kirkwood is not being sponsored for any of the content in this book.

John Kirkwood owns all image rights in this book.

John Kirkwood does not allow anyone to copy or use any of the images unless granted consent via written permission. If you would like to contact us on granting permission for any images in this book, you may contact the team via email at:

enquiries@profoodhomemade.com

# Professional
# Food Home
# Made

### Wonderful professional recipes from our work kitchens, that you can replicate in the comfort your own kitchen

### By
### John Kirkwood

# Acknowledgements

My first successful YouTube video, making French
baguettes at home, was a total fluke, as i was just trying to show a friend how to
make them in his own kitchen. I had no idea that the channel would become as
popular as it is today, and that is mainly due to my fantastic viewers, who have
stuck with me and have tuned in every week for the last few years.

I would also like to thank my friends on both the,
Patreon and PayPal platforms, who have enabled me to afford new ingredients
for all the recipes in my videos, and help with production costs. If it wasn't for
you kind people, the channels quality would have been significantly lower.

I would also like to thank my wife, Terina son Stephen, and good
friend Harvey, for all their help and support in writing this book.

You can view most recipes in this book, via video format on YouTube

www.youtube.com/user/jonboy2478
You can view any of my recipes in this book by scanning the
QR codes with your smart device.

# Contents

**Basic bread making rules to follow when replicating any of my bread recipe in this book.**

**1.** Stick to the recipe rigidly, the quantities and ingredients are very important, and carefully worked out for successful results.

**2.** Try to use digital scales, for all of the measurements, including weighing the water, converting to cups and measuring jugs is very uncertain, and inaccurate, but weighing the ingredients (including the water) is very accurate, and for international continuity, the gram is the best unit to choose. Also try to use bottled water, as tap water contains chlorine, and in certain ares, in can be very high, which will weaken, or even kill your yeast.

**3.** Use proper bread flour, with at least 12% protein, check the ingredients list on the side of the flour bag for the protein level, protein may show in grams per serving, but just work it out, it needs to be 12g of protein, per 100g of flour. Plain or all purpose flour, has a lower protein count, and is great for pastries, cakes, and biscuits, but is NOT strong enough for making bread.

**4.** Very important step. Check that your yeast is working, BEFORE you start any bread recipe.

**5.** Proofing times in this book may vary depending on the temperature of your location.

**6.** To test your yeast, add a ¼tsp / 1g from your batch of yeast to some warm sugared water, wait for 10 minutes, if it starts to bubble up, then your yeast is good to use, if it is not activating at all, then your batch of yeast is dead, and needs replacing.

# Crusty Bread Rolls

## Ingredients

500g / 18oz Strong white bread flour
340g /mls Lukewarm water / 40°C / 104°F
4g / 1tsp Instant or active dried yeast
8g / 1tsp Salt
6g / 1tsp Sugar

---

Crusty Bread rolls 68% Hydration

---

## Method

**1.** Add the sugar to the warm water, and stir, once dissolved, add the yeast and stir it in thoroughly, set it aside until it activates.

**2.** Add the salt to the flour and mix together in a separate bowl.

**3.** Once activated, add the water to the stand mixer bowl, start the machine on first speed, gradually add the flour and salt to the bowl.

**4.** Scrape down the sides of the bowl and knead the dough for 10 minutes.

**5.** If you are kneading this recipe by hand, add all of the ingredients to a bowl and partially mix it all together, tip it out onto your worktop and knead the dough for 10 minutes, then carry on with recipe.

**6.** Turn out the dough from the mixer, and form it into a ball, place it into a lightly oiled bowl, cover the bowl, and let it rise for a minimum of 1 hour in a warm draft-free spot, the dough should at least double in size (this may take longer depending on the temperature of your kitchen).

**7.** After the first proof, turn it out and repeat the process, but only allow it proof for 30 minutes this time.

**8.** Grease 1 large, or 2 small baking trays, with lard, butter, or shortening.

**9.** After the second proof, turn out the dough onto a floured worktop, and knock the dough back, and form it into a ball.

**10.** Divide the dough ball into 6 or 8 equal pieces, and form them into small balls, place them evenly spaced, on a floured bench, dust lightly with flour, cover them with a dry light weight cloth and let them rest for 5 minutes.

You can watch the full video recipe on YouTube, by scanning this QR code

**11.** After the 5 min rest period, gently roll each dough ball into an oval shape, and place them onto the prepared baking tray, make sure there is plenty of room in between them, dust lightly with flour and cover with a light-weight dry cloth, allow to proof or rise, for 20 minutes.

**12.** When there is only 10 minutes left on the proof, preheat your oven to 200°C / 390°F / of Gas mark 6, and place a tray of hot water, on the bottom shelf in the oven, the steam produced will give the finished rolls a crispy crust.

**13.** When the proofing time is up and the oven is up to temperature, use a bakers blade or Lame, and carefully score the top each roll.

**14.** Place the tray of rolls in the middle of the oven, and set your timer for 16 minutes, if you want a darker crust, add a further 2 minutes at a time, until you reach the desired colour.

**15.** Remove from the oven and allow to cool on a wire rack.

# Panini Sandwich Bread

## Ingredients

400g / 14oz Strong white bread flour
256g / 256mls Lukewarm water 40°C / 104°F
8g / ⅓oz Softened butter or Lard
6g / 1⅓tsp Instant or active dried yeast
8g / 1tsp Salt
12g / 2tsp Sugar

---

Panini Bread rolls 64% Hydration

---

## Method

**1.** Add the sugar to the warm water and stir, once dissolved, add the yeast and stir it in thoroughly, set it aside until it activates.

**2.** Add the flour and salt to the stand mixer bowl, and add the now activated yeast mixture, followed by the soft butter.

**3.** Using the dough hook attachment knead the dough for 10 minutes.

**4.** If you are kneading this recipe by hand, add all of the ingredients to a bowl and partially mix it all together, tip it out onto your worktop and knead the dough for 10 minutes, then carry on with recipe.

**5.** Turn out the dough from the mixer, and form it into a ball, and place it into a lightly oiled bowl, cover the bowl, and let it rise for at a minimum, of 1 hour, the dough should at least double in size (this may take longer depending on the temperature of your room).

**6.** Grease a large baking tray, I use a 30 x 30cm / 12 x 12in, non stick baking tray for this recipe.

**7.** Divide the dough ball into 4 equal pieces, and form them into small oval shapes, cover them and let them rest and relax for five minutes.

You can watch the full video recipe on YouTube, by scanning this QR code

**8.** After the five minutes, the dough pieces should be easy enough to form into long Panini shaped rolls.

**9.** Place the rolls on the greased baking tray, leaving room in-between them for them to rise without touching each other, cover with a dry light-weight cloth, and leave in a warm draft free spot, for 45 to 60 minutes.

**10.** When there is only 10 minutes left on the proof, preheat your oven to 190°C / 375°F / or Gas mark 5, and place a tray of hot water, on the bottom shelf in the oven, the steam produced will give the Panini rolls a tougher crust.

**11.** Soon as the oven is up to temperature, place the tray of rolls in the middle of the oven, and set your timer for 15 minutes.

**12.** When done, place them on a wire rack and allow to completely cool.

**13.** It's best to leave these rolls for a few hours before making your Panini sandwiches, in your Panini grill.

**12.** Cover the frying pan with a lightweight dry cloth and allow the dough balls to proof/rise for 30 minutes.

**13.** Prepare an egg-wash, with 1 small egg and a little milk.

**14.** When there's only 10 minutes left on the proof, preheat your oven to 190°C / 375°F / or Gas mark 5.

**15.** After the 30 min proof, brush the rolls with the egg wash, sprinkle on a little oregano, coarse sea salt, and freshly ground black pepper.

**16.** Place the pan in the hot oven, and set your timer for 25 minutes.

**17.** Halfway through the baking time, remove from the oven and brush again with the egg wash, return to the oven and bake for the remainder of the time.

**18.** Remove from the oven, place on a wire rack, and allow it to cool for 15 minutes.

**19.** Place the pan on the table next to a bowl of melted Camembert or Brie cheese, and allow your guests to tear share and dip.

# Garlic Bread
# Tear n Share

## Ingredients

400g / 14oz Strong white bread flour
248g / 248mls Warm water / 40°C / 104°F
10mls Vegetable oil
7g / 2tsp Instant or active dried yeast
6g / ½tsp Salt
6g / 1tsp Sugar
4g / 1tsp Garlic granules or powder
1g / ½tsp Dried Oregano
1 Egg (for egg wash)
Sea salt and black pepper for topping

---

Tear n Share Garlic Bread 62% Hydration

## Method

**1.** Add the sugar to the warm water and stir, once dissolved, add the yeast and stir it in thoroughly, set it aside until it activates.

**2.** Add the salt, dried oregano, and garlic granules to the flour, and mix together.

**3.** Once activated, add the yeast mixture to the stand mixer bowl, pour in the oil, add the flour mixture to the bowl.

**4.** Using the dough hook attachment start the machine on the slowest speed, and knead for 10 minutes.

**5.** If you are kneading this recipe by hand, add all of the ingredients to a bowl, and partially mix it all together, tip it out onto your worktop, and hand knead the dough for 10 minutes, then carry on with recipe.

**6.** Turn out the dough from the mixer, and form it into a ball, place it into a lightly oiled bowl, cover the bowl, and let it rise for a minimum of 1 hour in a warm draft-free spot, the dough should at least double in size (this time may vary, depending on the temperature of your kitchen)

**7.** After the first proof, turn it out and repeat the process, but only allow it to proof for 45 minutes this time.

**8.** Prepare a vessel for baking this recipe in, I like to use a well-greased, 23cm / 9in oven proof! frying pan, *(see image opposite:)*

**9.** After the second proof, turn out the dough onto a non-floured worktop, and knock the dough back, and form it into a ball.

**10.** Divide the dough ball into 16 equal pieces, and form those into small balls, placing them evenly spaced on a floured work surface.

**11.** Arrange the balls in the frying pan as so, 10 around the outer rim, then 5, and the last one goes in the middle.

You can watch the full video recipe on YouTube, by scanning this QR code

# Farmhouse Crusty Sandwich Loaf

## Ingredients

500g / 18oz Strong white bread flour
305g / 305mls Lukewarm water / 40°C / 104°F
7g / 2tsp Instant or active dried yeast
15g / ½oz Softened butter
8g / 1tsp Salt
6g / 1tsp Sugar

---

Farmhouse Crusty Loaf 61% Hydration

## Method

**1.** Add the sugar to the warm water and stir, once dissolved, add the yeast and stir it in thoroughly, set it aside until it activates.

**2.** In a bowl add the flour, add the salt and mix together, make a well in the flour.

**3.** Once activated, add the yeast mixture and the soft butter to the well in the bowl, mix together until you have a sticky dough.

**4.** Turn out the contents of the bowl onto your worktop, making sure you scrape down all of the flour, from the sides of the bowl.

**5.** Using your bench scraper, bring it all together, and hand knead the dough for 10 minutes.

**6.** If you wish to use a stand mixer, add all of the ingredients to the machines bowl, and knead for 10 minutes, using the dough hook attachment.

**7.** After the 10-minute kneading, form the dough into a ball, place it into a lightly oiled bowl, cover the bowl, let it rise for a minimum of 1 hour, in a warm draft-free spot, the dough should at least double in size (this may take longer depending on the temperature of your kitchen).

*Bakers Lame or blade*
*for scoring bread dough*

You can watch the full video recipe on YouTube, by scanning this QR code

**8.** Grease a 900g / 2lb loaf tin, the dimensions of the tin should be around 23 x 13 x 6.5cm  /  9 x 5 x 2½ inch.

**9.** After the I hour proofing, turn out the risen dough onto a non floured surface, and knock the dough back, this simply means force all of the gas out of it.

**10.** Form the dough into a sausage shape and place it in the greased loaf tin, gently pressing it down to fill in any gaps in the corners.

**11.** Lightly flour the top of the dough, then cover it with a dry light weight cloth, and allow it to proof until it has risen approximately 6cm / 2½ inches, over the top of the tin, this should take approx, 30 to 45 minutes.

**12.** When you think there is only 10 minutes left on the proof, preheat your oven to 180°C / 355°F or gas mark 4, at the same time, place a pan/dish of hot water on the bottom shelf of your oven, (the steam created will make the loaf top crispier).

**13.** Once the dough has fully risen, sprinkle on a little flour, and using your bakers Lame, or razor blade *(see image opposite)* carefully make a slash/cut down the full length and centre of the dough,  and get it into the preheated oven, and set your timer for 30 minutes.

**14.** After the 30 minutes remove it from the oven, immediately take it out of the tin, and place the loaf back in the oven, and increase the temperature to 210°C / 410°F / Gas mark 7, bake for a further 6 minutes.

**15.** Remove from the oven, allow to cool on a wire rack for 30 minutes, before slicing and serving.

# English Breakfast Muffins

## Ingredients

350g/12.3oz Strong white bread flour
4g / 1tsp instant or active dried yeast
6g / ¾tsp Salt
15g/½oz Sugar
15g / ½oz Butter (softened)
1 Large egg (beaten)
190g / mls Milk

English Muffins 70 % Hydration

## Method

**1.** Add the egg, milk, sugar and yeast to a jug, and thoroughly mix, set it aside for 10 minutes, until it activates and foams up.

**2.** Add the flour and salt to a large bowl, and mix together, then form a well in the middle.

**3.** Add the activated yeast mixture to the well, followed by the soft butter, mix it all together until you have a sticky dough, cover the bowl, and put it in a warm spot, to proof for 45 minutes.

**4.** When the proofing time is up, turn out the dough onto a floured surface, pour 1tsp of vegetable oil into the empty bowl, and spread it out, knock the dough back, form it into a ball and place it back into the oiled bowl, coat the dough in the oil, cover the bowl and proof it again for a further 45 minutes.

**5.** Prepare a baking tray, by sprinkling on some course semolina flour, or ordinary flour.

**6.** Turn out the dough onto a floured surface, carefully flatten it by hand, and using a rolling pin, roll it to approx 13mm / ½in thick.

**7.** Using a 7.5cm / 3in scone/pastry cutter, cut out 6 circles, place them on the prepared baking tray, roll the remainder of the dough into a ball, roll it out and cut a further 2 circles, you should now have 8 raw muffins.

**8.** Cover the muffins with a dry, light weight cloth, and proof in a warm spot, for 30 minutes.

**9.** Take a large frying pan or griddle, no oil, heat it up to approx 200°C / 390°F, and place 3 or 4 of the muffins in, and cook for 4 to 5 minutes on either side, once they are golden brown and firm to the touch, remove from the pan, and repeat the process with the others.

**10.** Storing and serving suggestions, once they are cooled, these can be frozen, you can take them out of the freezer in the morning, defrost in a couple of minutes, in the microwave on the defrost setting, cut in half,  toast, add lashings of butter and jam, or butter and a poached egg, resulting in delicious fresh hot muffins for breakfast.

You can watch the full video recipe on YouTube, by scanning this QR code

# Tiger Bread

## Ingredients

*For the Bread:*
450g / 16oz White bread flour
255g/mls Warm water (approx 40°C / 104°F)
6g / 1tsp Sugar
7g / 2 tsp instant or active dried yeast
8g / 1tsp Salt
15g / 1tbls Vegetable oil
*For the tiger topping:*
100g / 3½oz Rice flour
110g / mls Water
15g / 1tbls Sesame oil
2g / ½tsp Yeast
3g / ½tsp Sugar
2g / ½tsp Salt

---

### Tiger Bread 57% Hydration

## Method

**1.** Add the sugar and yeast to the warm water, mix well and allow the yeast to activate for 10 minutes, until it foams up.

**2.** Place the flour and salt into a bowl, and mix together.

**3.** Add all of the ingredients, including the oil, to the stand mixer bowl, and with the dough hook attached, knead for 12 minutes, on the slowest speed.

**4.** For hand kneading, add the yeast mixture to the flour, and add the oil, then mix the ingredients together in the bowl, tip the contents of the bowl out onto the bench, and bring it all together, and hand knead for 12 minutes.

**5.** After kneading, place the dough into a lightly oiled bowl, cover and allow to proof for 30 minutes in a warm, draft-free spot.

**6.** After the 30 minutes, turn it out onto your workbench, and knock it back, form it into a ball.

**7.** Get it back into the bowl, and allow it to proof for 45 minutes this time.

**8.** Grease a large baking tray with oil, butter, or lard.

**9.** In a small bowl, mix together all of the tiger topping ingredients, and set it aside to proof for now.

**10.** After the 45 minute proof on the bread dough, turn out the dough once more, dust with a little flour, and knock it back, form it into a ball and place the dough ball in the centre of the prepared baking tray, lightly flour the dough, cover it with a lightweight dry cloth, and allow it to rise in a warm spot, for a further 45 minutes.

**11.** Once the final time is up, preheat your oven to 190° / 375°F / Gas mark 5, place a pan of hot water on the bottom shelf of the oven, the steam produced, will make the bread crispy.

**12.** The the tiger topping mix should be active by this time, give it a good whisk, until it is a smooth paste.

**13.** Once the bread dough has fully risen, remove the cover from the dough, and very carefully, using a pastry brush, brush the tiger topping mixture all over the surface of the dough, *(see image: opposite)*.

**14.** Place the tray into the preheated oven, and set your timer for 35 minutes.

**15.** Once the time is up, remove the tiger bread, and place it on a wire rack to cool.

**16.** Once cool, slice and serve with butter.

You can watch the full video recipe on YouTube, by scanning this QR code

# Vietnamese Baguette Banh Mi

## Ingredients

525g /18½oz Strong white bread flour
390g / 390mls Water
1tsp / 8g Salt
2g / ½tsp Instant or active dried yeast

---

6 Vietnamese baguettes 74% Hydration

---

## Method

**1.** Start the recipe by adding the flour, yeast, and salt to a bowl, mix these dry ingredients together, add the water and bring it all together to a sticky shaggy dough, see *(Fig1)* opposite.

**2.** Cover the bowl, and set your timer for 45 minutes.

**3.** After the 45 minutes, turn the dough out onto a none floured, slightly wet surface, and with wet hands knock the dough back, by giving it 5 or 6 turns.

**4.** Place the dough back in the bowl, cover and allow to proof for 1 hour, in a warm draft-free spot.

**5.** After the 1 hour proofing, the dough should have at least, doubled in size, turn out the dough onto a floured surface, then divide the dough into 6 equal pieces, and pre-shape them as shown in *(Fig 2)* opposite, cover them with a piece of oiled cling film / plastic wrap, see *(Fig 3)* opposite, and let them rest and relax for 20 minutes.

**6.** After the 20 minutes rest, lightly oil the worktop, and form the pre-shapes into a triangle, see *(Fig 4)* opposite, and starting from the thin end, gradually roll the dough back towards you, see *(Fig 5)* until you get the shape as shown in *(Fig 6)*, to get a good seal on the base, nip the bottom seam together with your fore fingers and thumbs.

**7.** Once all 6 baguettes are formed, transfer them to a Couche cloth, see (Fig 6) (I use a white cotton pillowcase, see Fig 6) , or you cau use a perforated metal baguette baking tray (See image below), either way, give them a good dusting of flour, and cover with a dry, lightweight cloth, allow then to rise for 30 minutes.

**8.** When there is only 10 minutes left on the final proof, pre heat your oven to 220°C that's 430°F or Gas mark 7,  at the same time, place a pan of hot water on the bottom shelf of the oven.

**9.** If you used the Couche cloth method, carefully transfer the baguettes to a lightly greased baking tray, and score the baguettes 2 or 3 times, place them in the preheated oven.

**10.** If you are using a baguette baking tray, slash the baguettes, and simply place the tray into the hot oven, spray inside the oven with water using a fine mist spray bottle, , and bake for 16 minutes, if you prefer yours a little browner, bake for 18 minutes.

**11.** Remove from the oven and place on a wire rack until cool.

Perforated Baguette
baking tray

You can watch the full video recipe on YouTube, by scanning this QR code

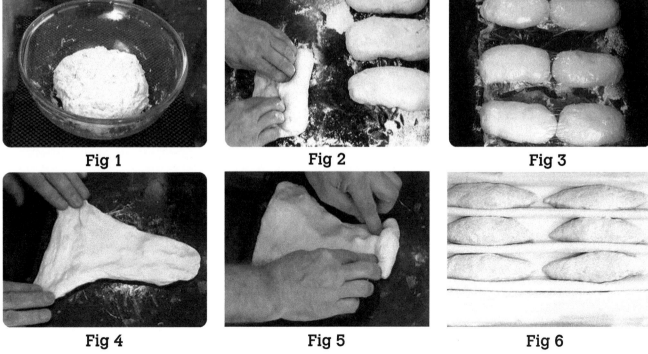

Fig 1

Fig 2

Fig 3

Fig 4

Fig 5

Fig 6

# Cottage Loaf

## Ingredients

500g / 18oz White bread flour
260g/mls Warm water (approx 40°C / 104°F)
7g / 2 tsp instant or active dried yeast
8g / 1tsp Salt
20g Vegetable oil or soft butter
6g / 1tsp Sugar

Cottage Loaf 52% Hydration

## Method

**1.** Add the sugar and yeast to the warm water, mix well, and allow the yeast to activate for 10 minutes, or until it foams up.

**2.** Place the flour and salt into a bowl, and mix together.

**3.** Add all of the ingredients, including the oil, to the stand mixer bowl, and with the dough hook attached, knead for 10 minutes, on the slowest speed.

**4.** For hand kneading, add the yeast mixture to the flour, and add the oil, then mix the ingredients together in the bowl, tip the contents of the bowl out onto the bench, and bring it all together, and hand knead for 10 minutes.

**5.** After kneading, place the dough into a lightly oiled bowl, cover and allow to proof for 60 minutes, in a warm draft-free spot.

**6.** Grease a large baking tray.

**7.** After the 60 minutes proofing time, turn it out onto your workbench, and knock it back, this simply means push all of the gas out of it.

**8.** If your measurements were correct at the start, your dough should weigh approximately 800g / 28oz, cut off 200g / 7oz, of the dough, then form both pieces into 2 dough balls.

**9.** Place the large dough ball in the centre of the prepared baking tray, and flatten it down a little, place the smaller ball, on top and in the middle of the larger one.

**10.** Take a wooden spoon and dip the handle into some flour, push the handle straight down the middle of both dough balls, all the way to the bottom, and gently pull it out again, this action, ties both balls together.

**11.** Dust the loaf with flour, cover with a dry lightweight cloth, and proof for 30 minutes to one hour, depending on the temperature of your location.

**12.** Once you think there is only 10 minutes left on the proofing time, add a pan of water to the bottom of your oven, then set your temperature to 200°C / 392°F / Gas mark 6.

**13.** Make a few slashes in the dough, similar to the image below, or see the video, via the QR code at the bottom of this page *(see image opposite)*.

**14.** Place the tray into the preheated oven and set your timer for 30 minutes.

**15.** Once the time is up, remove it from the oven, and allow it cool on a wire rack for 20 minutes, slice and serve with butter.

You can watch the full video recipe on YouTube, by scanning this QR code

**13.** Place the tray/trays in the preheated oven, and set your timer for 20 minutes.

**14.** Once the time is up, remove the bread from the oven, add a little grated cheese on the top of each loaf, place them back in the oven, without the tray this time, and bake for a further 5 minutes.

**15.** Remove from the oven and onto a wire rack and allow to cool for 15 minutes, before slicing and serving.

**16.** One of the loaves can be frozen, to use at a later date, but freeze immediately after it has cooled from the oven,

No Knead Recipe

# Jalapeño Chilli & Cheese Bread

## Ingredients

450g / 16½oz Strong white bread flour
324g / 324mls Lukewarm water / 40°C / 104°F
100g / 3½oz mature/sharp cheese
35g / 1½oz Jalapeño or Mixed chillies
4g / 1tsp Instant or active dried yeast
8g / 1tsp Salt
6g / 1tsp Sugar
Extra cheese for topping

---

### Chilli & Cheese bread 72% Hydration

## Method

**1.** Add the sugar and yeast, to the warm water, mix well and allow the yeast to activate for 10 minutes, or until it foams up.

**2.** Finely chop the Jalapeño chillies, and weigh off your grated cheese, I personally recommend a good mature cheddar, for this recipe.

**3.** Add the chopped chillies, grated cheese, and salt to the flour in a large mixing bowl, and mix together well.

**4.** Pour in the yeast mixture, and thoroughly mix until you have a sticky, shaggy dough, *(See image opposite)*.

**5.** Cover the bowl, and allow to proof for 45 minutes.

**6.** Turn out the dough onto a slightly wet surface, and with wet hands, fold the dough 4 or 5 times, place it back into the bowl, cover, and proof for a further 45 minutes.

**7.** Once the time is up, repeat the previous procedure exactly, these rest and rise periods are very important to get the best taste, and texture in this style of bread.

**8.** Grease 1 large, or 2 small baking trays.

**9.** After the 3rd and final 45-minute proof in the bowl, turn out the dough onto a floured surface, knock it back again, then divide it into 2 pieces, form each piece into an oval shaped loaf, allow the dough to rest for 5 minutes.

**10.** Place the 2 loaves on the prepared baking tray/trays, sprinkle on a little flour, cover with a lightweight dry cloth, and allow to proof and rise for 40 minutes.

**11.** When there's only 10 minutes left on the proof, preheat your oven to 210°C / 410°F / Gas mark 7, and place a tray of hot water on the bottom shelf of your oven, the steam produced, will give the loaves a crispy crust.

**12.** When the 40 minute proofing time is up, score the loaves down the middle, using a razor blade, or bakers Lame, *(see image on page 10)*

You can watch the full video recipe on YouTube by scanning this code

# Apple Crumble

## Ingredients

**Crumble mix:**
170g / 6oz Plain / all-purpose flour
100g / 3½oz Soft brown sugar
45g / 1½oz Oats / Oatmeal
2g / ½tsp Ground Cinnamon
1g / ¼tsp Nutmeg
100g / 3½oz Butter

**Filling:**
1kg / 2¼lb Apples of your choice
1 Medium lemon, Zest and juice
45g / 1½oz Sugar
45g / 1½oz Butter
1g / ¼tsp Ground Cinnamon

Serves Approximately 6

## Method

**1.** Start the recipe by finely grating the zest, and juicing 1 medium size lemon.

**2.** Wash, peel, core, and dice the apples, into about 13mm / ½in pieces, once all the apples are diced, coat them with lemon juice and set them aside for now.

**3.** Making the crumble mix, add the flour, Sugar, Oats, spices and butter to a bowl, and slowly start to rub the ingredients together with your fingers, until you have a course breadcrumb consistency, once your crumble mix is made, set that aside until needed, the fridge is a good place to store it.

**4.** Preheat your oven to 180°C / 356°F / gas mark 4.

**5.** Add the sugar from the filling ingredients list, to a large hot frying pan or wok, when it dissolves and starts to turn a golden brown colour, carefully add the apples.

**6.** Cook and continually stir the apples for a couple of minutes, add the lemon zest and Cinnamon, and mix in, finally add the butter, stir and cook for a further 3 minutes.

**7.** Transfer the cooked hot apples to a suitable baking pan, or ceramic dish *(see video for examples and sizes, scan the QR code opposite with your smart phone or tablet to view the video recipe)* and level them off,  the evenly cover the apples with the crumble mix, then get it into the hot oven, and set your timer for 40 minutes.

**8.** When the time is up, remove from the oven, and let it relax on a wire rack for a minute or two , serve piping hot, with fresh cream, ice cream, or my particular favourite, vanilla custard, *(see bonus recipe opposite)*.

You can watch the full video recipe on YouTube, by scanning this QR code

# Egg & Vanilla Custard

## Method

**1.** Start the recipe by separating 5 room temperature egg yolks.

**2.** Heat the milk, vanilla extract, and cream in a suitable saucepan, on a low to medium heat, bring to a simmer.

**3.** Meanwhile, whisk the egg yolks and sugar, until the colour turns a pale yellow, this takes approx 1 minute.

**4.** Add the corn flour/starch to the egg mixture and whisk in.

**5.** Pour 2 ladles of the hot milk/cream from the saucepan, onto the egg mixture, and quickly whisk it in, this is to temper the eggs.

**6.** Now add the egg mixture, to the rest of the liquid in the saucepan, and very slowly bring it back to a simmer on a low heat, stirring continuously.

**7.** Once the custard thickens, it is ready to serve.

You can watch the full video recipe on YouTube, by scanning this QR code

## Ingredients

300mls Milk
300mls Double or heavy cream
5 Egg yolks
70g / 2½oz Granulated sugar
2tsp / 12mls Vanilla extract
½tsp Corn flour / starch

# Sticky Toffee Pudding With a Creamy Treacle Sauce

## Ingredients

200g / 7oz Stoned dates
250g / mls Water
175g / 6oz Plain or all purpose flour
175g / 6oz Granulated sugar
60g / 2oz Soft unsalted butter
2 large beaten eggs
4g / 1tsp Bicarbonate of soda / Baking soda
2g / ½tsp Baking powder
6mls / 1tsp Vanilla extract
*Creamy Black Treacle Sauce:*
300mls double or Heavy cream
40g / 2tbls Black treacle or Blackstrap molasses
15g / 1tbls Soft brown sugar
6mls / 1tsp Vanilla extract

## Serves Approximately 6

## Method

**1.** Stone and cut the dates into small pieces (once stoned, you need a finished weight of 200g /7oz of dates)

**2.** In a small, but fairly deep saucepan, add the water followed by the chopped dates, bring it to a light boil, and let them simmer for 3 minutes.

**3.** When the times up turn off the heat, remove it altogether if you're on an electric hob, then add the bicarbonate of soda, you may know that as baking soda, give it a good whisk, it will fizz up some, this is why you need a deepish pan, the soda brings it all together into a sticky mass, and that's what puts the sticky, in sticky toffee pudding, allow the mixture to cool.

*Top pro tip:* to cool something like these dates quickly, is to carefully float you saucepan in a sink of cold water, it will reduce the cooling time considerably.

**4.** Grease and flour a 900g / 2lb loaf tin, the dimensions of the tin are 23 x 13 x 6.5cm / 9 x 5 x 2½ inch.

**5.** Preheat your oven to 170°C / 340°F / Gas mark 3.

**7.** Time to make the cake batter, add the butter and sugar to a large mixing bowl, using a spatula or a hand mixer, cream them together until you have a smooth creamy mixture, add the eggs and vanilla extract, and thoroughly mix together.

**8.** Sift in the flour and baking powder, and gently fold it all together.

**9.** Add the now cooled sticky date mixture to the batter, and gently fold it all together.

**10.** Carefully pour the mixture into the prepared loaf tin/pan, give the tin a couple of gentle taps on the bench, to lift any large air bubbles, and get it into the preheated oven, and bake for 1 hour .

**11.** When the time is up on the pudding, carefully test it with a cocktail stick, if it comes out clean, it's done, if not, give it an extra 5 minutes, and test it again, remove from the oven, allow it to settle for 10 minutes on a wire rack, before removing it from the tin.

**12.** ***Black Treacle Sauce:*** Time to make the sauce: in a small saucepan, on a medium heat, add the 300mls or half pint of double or heavy cream, followed by the brown sugar, and the half teaspoon of vanilla extract, whisk together, and slowly bring it up to a simmer, once hot, add the black treacle, continue whisking until the sauce begins to boil and thicken, stop at that point and remove from the heat.

**13.** Carefully remove the pudding from the tin, slice and serve while still hot, with plenty of that delicious thick and creamy treacle sauce, and vanilla ice cream.

You can watch the full video recipe on YouTube, by scanning this QR code

# Sherry Trifle

## Ingredients

**Jelly:**
100g / 3½oz Plain sponge or a small Madeira cake
60mls / 4tbls Cream Sherry (Optional)
25g strawberry jelly crystals + 570mls / 1pt boiling water
150g / 5oz Strawberries
150g / 5oz Raspberries

**Custard:**
25g / 1oz Custard powder
570mls / 1pt milk
25g / 1oz Sugar
6mls / 1tsp Vanilla extract

**Chantilly cream:**
280mls / ½pt Double or heavy whipping cream
6mls / 1tsp Vanilla extract
12g / 2tsp Icing or powdered sugar

---

### Makes 4 Individual trifles

## Method

### *Jelly Stage:*

**1.** Wash and cut half of the fruit into smaller pieces, place in a bowl, and add ½ tsp of sugar, and mix.

**2.** Make up your pint of jelly.

**3.** Cube, and place 25g of your sponge in each of your standard size wine glasses, just covering the bottom of your glasses.

**4.** Add 1 dessert spoon, 15mls of Sherry to each glass, (optional).

**5.** Divide your cut fruit into the glasses, do not fill above the halfway mark of each glass.

**6.** Pour in the jelly until it reaches the top of the fruit, halfway up the glasses, that you are using *(see image opposite)*.

**7.** Place all 4 glasses in the fridge, for at least 2 hours, until the jelly completely sets.

### *Custard:*

**8.** Don't start the custard, until you are sure, the jelly has fully set.

**9.** Add the custard powder, sugar, and vanilla, to a saucepan, pour in a little of the cold milk, thoroughly whisk, once smooth, add the rest of the milk and mix.

**10.** Turn on the heat, and slowly bring to a steady gentle boil, soon as it is thick, remove from the heat and pour it into a heatproof jug. *(For traditional homemade vanilla custard: see recipe on page 23)*

**11.** Pour about 13mm / ½in of the hot custard, onto the top of your set jelly, place them back in the fridge, until the custard has completely set.

### *Chantilly cream:*

**12.** Add the whipping cream, vanilla extract, sugar, to a bowl, and whisk until the cream thickens to stiff peaks, cover and refrigerate, using an electric hand or stand mixer, this should take around 3 to 4 minutes.

**13.** Spoon the whipped cream onto the set custard, leaving it shy of the top of the glass.

**14.** Finish off the tops using the rest of your fruit, *(see opposite for design ideas)*.

**15.** You can also add whatever decoration you prefer to the top of the fruit too.

**16.** Place in the fridge until needed, these can be made hours in advance of serving them.

You can watch the full video recipe on YouTube, by scanning this QR code

# Individual Scotch Pies

## Ingredients

### The Pastry:

400g / 14oz Plain or all-purpose flour
160g / mls Water
90g / 3½oz Butter
100g / 3½oz Lard or shortening
8g / 1tsp Salt
Egg wash

### The Filling:

500g / 18oz Minced/ground Lamb
1 Medium size onion, finely diced
2tbls Olive oil
4g / 1tsp Ground Mace
2g / 1tsp mixed herbs
2 Small Bay leaves (optional)
Salt and pepper to taste
570mls / 1 Pint Beef or lamb stock

---

Makes 4 Individual Pies

---

## Method

### Making the pastry:

**1** Place the water on a low heat, and add the butter and lard to the pan, bring to a simmer.

**2.** Mix the salt and flour together in a bowl, and make a well in the centre.

**3.** Soon as the fats have melted, pour the hot liquid into the flour well in the bowl, and bring it roughly together.

**4.** Tip the contents of the bowl out onto a floured worktop, and gently hand knead the pastry, until it all comes together.

**5.** Cut the pastry into 2 pieces, 2 thirds, for the base of the pies, and 1 third, for the tops of the pies.

**6.** Cover in plastic wrap or food bags, and place in the fridge for at least 1 hour before using it.

### Making the filling:

**7.** Heat up the oil in a medium size pan that has a lid, add the diced onions, and fry until soft.

**8.** Add the spices and seasoning to the pan, and stir them in, add the minced lamb, and fry until the mince has broken down to smaller pieces, and has coloured.

**9.** Add the beef stock to the pan, for extra flavour, you can add a couple of Bay leaves at this point, bring to a slow boil, place the lid on the pan, and simmer for 10 minutes.

**10.** Once done, strain off the stock, add the mince to a separate bowl, cover it, and allow it to cool.

**11.** Pour the stock into a jug, and skim off the fat while it's still hot.

**12.** This recipe will make 4 small individual pies, pie dish dimensions should be 10 x 2cm or 4 x 1 inches.

**13.** Roll out your pastry to approx 3mm thick, and cut out 4, 12.5cm / 5in circles for the bases of the pies, and 4, 10cm / 4in circles, for the lids of the pies, also cut a small vent hole in the lids, *(See image below)*.

**14.** Place the pastry bases in the lightly greased pie tins, press the pastry right down into the corners, make sure you leave some pastry sticking over the rim of the pie tin.

**15.** Fill the cases with the Lamb mincemeat, lightly compact it down, and fill right to the top.

**16.** Brush egg wash all around the edge of the pastry in the tin, place on the lid of the pie, and crimp the pastry together all around the edge of the pies.

**17.** Preheat your oven to, 170°C / 340°F / Gas mark 3.

**18.** Place all 4 pies on a baking tray, give each pie a good coat of the egg wash.

**19.** Place the tray in the preheated oven, set your timer for 40 minutes.

*Making the Gravy:*

**20.** Pour the stock from the jug that was made earlier, into a small saucepan, bring to a simmer, add a couple of knobs of butter, (this will give the gravy a nice glaze).

**21.** To thicken the gravy, mix 1 tsp of cornflour/starch in 2 tbls of cold water, add it to the simmering gravy a little at a time while stirring, until you reach the required thickness that you like.

**22.** Simmer on a very low heat for 5 minutes, with the lid on, and that is your tasty gravy done.

**23.** When the time is up, remove the pies from the oven, place the tray on a wire rack for 5 minutes.

**24.** Carefully remove hot pies from the tins, and serve immediately, with peas and mashed potatoes or fries, and lots of that delicious gravy.

You can watch the full video recipe on YouTube, by scanning this QR code

You can watch the full video recipe on YouTube, by scanning this QR code

# Salmon & Broccoli Mini Quiche

## Ingredients

*The Hot water crust Pastry:*
300g / 11oz Plain or All-purpose flour
120g / 120mls Water
70g / 2½oz Butter
70g / 2½oz Lard or shortening
4g / ½tsp Salt
*The filling:*
6 Large eggs
50g / 50mls Milk
250g / 9oz Salmon fillet
90g /3oz Broccoli
100g / 3½oz Grated mature/sharp cheddar cheese
2 Spring/green onions
Salt & Pepper to taste

Makes 12 small quiches

## Method

*Making the pastry:*

**1** Place the water on a low heat, then add the butter and lard to the pan, bring to a simmer.

**2.** Mix the salt and flour together in a bowl, and make a well in the centre.

**3.** Soon as the fats have melted, pour the hot liquid into the flour well in the bowl, and bring it roughly together.

**4.** Tip the contents of the bowl out onto a floured worktop, and gently hand knead the pastry, until it all comes together.

**5.** Cover in plastic wrap, or food bags, and place in the fridge for at least 1 hour before using it.

*Preparing the filling:*

**6.** Prepare the filling starting with the broccoli, use the small floret tips only, don't add the tougher stems, and finely chop the spring onions.

**7.** Dice the salmon into 13mm that's ½in cubes.

**8.** Whisk the eggs together in a jug, then add the milk, whisk again for a couple of moments to incorporate plenty of air, you may season the mixture with salt and pepper at this point.

**9.** Once chilled, roll out the pastry into a 3mm thick sheet, and cut out twelve, 10cm / 4in circles.

**10.** Line each cup, of a well greased, standard size muffin tin, with the pastry circles, leaving a little sticking over the top, as the pastry will shrink some when baking.

**11.** Preheat your oven to 180°C / 355°F / Gas mark 4.

**12.** Time to build up the layers of the quiche, start by adding a little of the egg mixture to each cup, approx 6mm / ¼in, and add a pinch of the grated cheese to the cup too, this should use about half, of your cheeese.

**13.** Add a good pinch of the spring onions to the cups, followed by 3 or 4 pieces of the salmon.

**14.** Now divide all the broccoli into each cup, followed by the rest of the spring onions, now add the rest of the salmon pieces.

**15.** Add the remainder of the egg mixture, filling each cup, to just below the surface.

**16.** Finally add the rest of the grated cheese to each cup.

**17.** Place the muffin tray in the preheated oven, and set your timer, for 30 minutes.

**18.** Remove from the oven, allow to cool on a wire rack for 10 minutes, before carefully removing them from the muffin cups.

**19.** These delicious mini quiches, can be served hot or cold.

# Steak & Kidney Pie

## Ingredients

### The Pastry:
340g / 12oz Plain or all purpose flour
85g / 3oz cold butter
85g / 3oz cold lard or shortening
½tsp Salt
115mls / 115g / 4 oz of cold water
1 small egg beaten with a dash of milk (egg-wash)

### The Pie Filling:
900g / 2lb of lean diced beef
4 Lamb kidneys approx 200g / 7oz (chopped small)
1 medium size onion (diced)
1 pint of stock: chicken or beef
Small bunch of Thyme leaves, or 1 tsp dried Thyme
2 beef stock cubes
30g / 1oz Corn flour/starch
30g / 1oz Cold water

### Serves Approximately 6

## Method

### *Making the pastry:*

**1.** Add the flour, salt, cold butter and lard to a food processor, pulse until it resembles fine breadcrumbs, add the cold water, when the pastry forms into a ball, it is done, this should only take about 45 seconds.

**2.** Cut the pastry in half, form each half into a puck shape, wrap in plastic wrap, and place in the fridge for at least 30 minutes, or until needed.

**3.** To make the pastry by hand: add the flour, salt, cold butter, and lard to a bowl, rub the ingredients together until there is no more lumps of fat, form a well in the middle, add the water, and cut it together using an ordinary dinner knife, gently knead the dough by hand, until it comes together, try not over work the pastry.

### *Making the filling:*

**4.** Cut and dice the onion into medium to small pieces.

**5.** Cut and dice the kidneys into small pieces, and refrigerate for now.

**6.** In a medium size pan, fry the onions, until soft, add the diced beef to the pan, and cover with the pint of (beef or chicken) stock, for extra flavour, crumble in 1 or 2 stock cubes, mix together before placing in the bunch of thyme leaves. Do not add the kidney yet.

**7.** Bring the ingredients to a slow boil, put on the pan lid, turn down the heat, and simmer for 1 hour, or until the meat is tender, as some cuts of beef may take longer, *at this point, you can add the kidney.*

**8.** Mix the corn flour and cold water together.

**9.** Once the meat is tender, ladle out the stock into another saucepan, (you can make the gravy from this, just bring to a boil, add some of the cornflour mixture to thicken) leaving about an inch in the pan, place back on the heat, and stir in a third of the corn flour mixture, stir until thick, set it aside until cool.

### *Putting the pie together:*

**10.** Preheat your oven to 190°C that's 375°F or gas mark 5, and grease a 20cm / 8" pie dish or pan.

**11.** Roll each pastry big enough to fit the pie tin, *(see video for rolling technique, scan the video QR code opposite).*

**12.** Place the bottom pastry in the greased tin carefully pushing it down into the corners, Prick the base of the pastry with a fork, (see right image).

**13.** Add the now cooled steak and kidney filling to the pastry base, and level it off.

**14.** Brush egg-wash or water, around edge of the rim, before adding the top pastry.

**15.** Crimp the edges together (*see right image for crimping technique)* trim off the excess pastry.

**16.** Brush the top of the pie with the egg-wash, prick in a few vent holes, using a fork.

**17.** Get the pie into the preheated oven, and set your kitchen timer, for 25 minutes.

**18.** Check when the time is up, if it's a shiny golden brown colour, it's done, if it's still a little pale, give it another 5 minutes, remember the filling is already cooked, you just need to concentrate on getting the pastry correct.

**19.** Remove from the oven, let it relax for 10 minutes before serving.

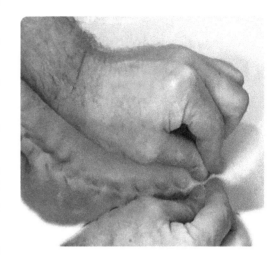

You can watch the full video recipe on YouTube, by scanning this QR code

# Chicken Curry Pie

## Ingredients

### The Pastry:
340g / 12oz Plain or All-purpose flour
85g / 3oz cold butter
85g / 3oz cold lard or shortening
60mls / 60g / 2 oz of cold water
1 Large egg
½tsp / 2g Salt

### The Filling:
600g / 21oz Chicken breasts diced small
1 Large onion, finely chopped
3 Cloves garlic, finely chopped
2tbls Olive oil
1g / ½tsp black pepper
4g / ½tsp Salt
100mls double cream + 50mls water
20g /2tbls Corn flour/starch in 20mls cold water
8g / 2tsp garam masala
4g / 1tsp Turmeric
2g / ½tsp hot chilli powder (add extra if needed)
Bunch of Coriander (optional)

### Serves Approximately 6

## Method

### Making the pastry:

**1.** Add the flour, salt, cold butter and lard to a food processor, pulse until it resembles fine breadcrumbs, add the cold water, when the pastry forms into a ball, it is done, this should only take about 45 seconds.

**2.** Cut the pastry in half, form each half into a puck shape, wrap in plastic wrap / cling film, and place in the fridge for at least 30 minutes, or until needed.

**3.** To make the pastry by hand: add the flour, salt, cold butter, and lard to a bowl, rub the ingredients together until there is no more lumps of fat, form a well in the middle, add the water, and cut it together using an ordinary dinner knife, gently knead the dough by hand, until it comes together, try not over work the pastry.

### Making the filling:

**4.** Add the oil to a large pan, and fry the onion until soft and just starting to colour.

**5.** Add the garlic, black pepper, and salt, stir.

**6.** Add the chicken and spices, mix it thoroughly with the onions.

**7.** Continuously stir-fry for approx 4 minutes, until the chicken starts to colour, and release its juices, now add the cream and cornflour mixture, once it has thickened, stir in the coriander, take off the heat and allow to cool.

### Making the Pie:

**8.** Preheat your oven to 170°C that's 340°F or gas mark 3.

**9.** Roll each pastry big enough to fit the pie tin, (see video for rolling technique, scan the video QR code below).

**10.** Place the bottom pastry into the greased tin carefully pushing it down into the corners.

**11.** Add the filling and level it off, try to dome the mixture so the middle is slightly higher than the edges.

**12.** Brush egg wash around edge of the rim, before adding the top pastry.

You can watch the full video recipe on YouTube, by scanning this QR code

**13.** Crimp the edges or the pastry together, (see video for crimping technique, scan the video QR code opposite). trim off the excess pastry.

**14.** Brush the top of the pie with the egg wash, prick in a few vent holes using a fork.

**15.** Get the pie into the preheated oven, and set your timer for 35 to 40 minutes, check when the time is up, if it's a shiny golden brown colour, it's done, if it's still a little pale, give it another 5 minutes.

**16.** Remove from the oven, let it relax for 10 minutes before slicing and serving.

# Easy Puff Pastry

## Ingredients

300g / 11oz Plain or all-purpose flour
250g / 8.8oz Cold unsalted butter
125g /mls Cold water
4g / ½tsp Salt
6mls / 1tsp Lemon or lime juice

---

### Makes Approximately 675g

## Method

**1.** Start by cutting off ⅓, that's 83g of the 250g pack of cold butter, and dice into small cubes.

**2.** Add the flour and salt, to a large bowl, and mix together.

**3.** Add the diced butter to the flour, rub together with your fingers until all the butter lumps are gone, and you should be left with a sandy consistency, in colour, and texture.

**4.** Add the water and lemon juice to the bowl, and roughly mix together, the lemon juice makes the dough more elastic, making it easier to roll, and helps the separation of the layers, when baking.

**5.** Turn out the mixture onto your worktop, and pull it all together with your hands, the mix will appear dry at first, but don't be tempted to add more water, it will come together eventually.

**6.** Form the dough into a rectangle, wrap in cling-film or plastic food bag, and refrigerate for 1 hour, *(see image 1. below)*

**7.** Take the remaining butter, and place it in-between 2 pieces of parchment paper, and using your rolling pin, form the butter into a 12cm or 5inch square, *(see image 2. opposite)* once done, place the butter in the fridge, for 30 to 45 minutes.

**8.** Take the now chilled pastry from the fridge, and on a floured surface, roll it out into a 30 x 18cm or 12 x 7in rectangle.

**9.** Remove the paper from the butter and place it on the top half of the pastry, leaving a small edge around the top and sides, *(see image 3. opposite)*.

**10.** Fold the bottom half of the pastry over the butter, and gently press down the edges, to form a parcel.

**11.** Turn the pastry parcel 90° to the left, and roll in out into a 30 x 18cm or 12 x 7inch rectangle once more.

*Image: 1*

You can watch the full video recipe on YouTube, by scanning this QR code

**12.** Brush off any excess flour, then carefully fold the bottom of the pastry up by ⅓, and fold the top down by one ⅓, gently pat it down, *(see image 4. below)* and using your parchment papers, neatly wrap it up and place it in the refrigerator for 20 minutes.

**13.** After it has chilled, (always on a floured surface) roll out the pastry once more into a 30 x 18cm or 12 x 7in rectangle, once again fold it exactly the same as the last time, bottom ⅓ up, top ⅓ down, wrap it in the parchment paper, and refrigerate for 20 minutes *(see image 5. below)*.

**14.** Repeat this procedure another 2 times, for a total of 4 roll and folds, chilling for 20 minutes each time, what is happening, each time you go through this procedure, the layers are building up in the pastry.

**15.** After the 4th, and final roll and fold, the pastry is ready to use, wrap the finished pastry in cling-film, and refrigerate, it will keep in the fridge for several days, or you can freeze it for future use.

**16.** You now have a beautiful, and very versatile delicious, buttery, puff pastry, that you can use in many recipes, including pies, pasties, sausage rolls, and including lots dessert recipes, it has many uses.

**17.** You can see this very pastry being used in my next recipe, a delicious Steak pasties. *(on page 38)*

*Steak Pasty recipe: Page 38*

*Image: 2*

*Image: 3*

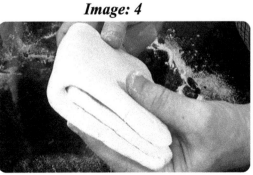

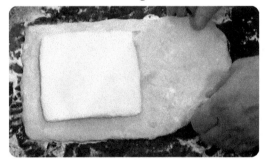

*Image: 4*

*Image: 5*

# Steak Pasties

## Ingredients

*To make the Puff pastry:*
*(See: Page 36)*

*Pasty filling:*
400g / 14oz Lean Stewing or Casserole beef
1 Small onion (finely chopped)
285mls / ½ Pint Beef stock
Salt and white pepper to taste
6mls / 1tsp Worcestershire sauce (optional)
2 Small Bay leaves (optional)
20g / 2Tbls Gravy granules
2tbls Olive or vegetable oil
1 Small egg, with a dash of milk, for the egg-wash

---

### Makes 4 Steak Pasties

## Method

### Making the filling:

**1.** Dice the stewing or casserole beef, into 13mm / ½inch cubes, and finely chop the oninon.

**2.** Place a medium size saucepan on a medium to high heat, and add the olive oil, once hot, add the onion and fry until soft.

**3.** Add the diced beef to the pan, and fry until it has a little colour, this should take around 5 minutes.

**4.** Pour in your beef stock, and bring to a simmer.

**5.** Season with salt and white pepper to taste, add the Worcestershire sauce, and the bay leaves.

**6.** Put on the lid, and on your very lowest heat, simmer for 1 to 1½ hours, or until the meat is tender.

**7.** Once tender, thicken the stew with the gravy granules, and allow the filling to completely cool.

### Preparing the puff pastry:

**8.** *See page 36:* on how to make puff pastry from scratch, or, it is perfectly acceptable, to use store bought puff pastry for the recipe too.

**9.** Roll out your pastry into a rectangle sheet 35 x 25cm or 14 x 10in, approx 4mm thick, out of that large sheet, cut out 4 pieces, 17.5 x 12.5cm or 7 x 5in.

**10.** Place each sheet on a slightly larger piece of floured parchment paper, stacked and refrigerated.

**11.** Take one sheet of pastry at a time, from the refrigerator, keeping it on the paper.

**12.** Add some filling to one side of the pastry, leaving a 13mm or ½in gap around the edge.

**13.** Brush the egg wash all around the exposed pastry, fold the pastry over the filling, gently press all of the air out of it, and seal around the edge using a fork, this also leaves a pleasing pattern around the edges of the pasty.

**14.** Place the pasty, whilst still on the parchment paper, onto a baking tray, repeat for the other 3 pasties.

**15.** At this point, preheat your oven to, 170°C / 340°F / Gas mark 3.

**16.** Give each pasty a good coat of the egg wash, and cut 3 small vents in each one, using a sharp knife.

**17.** Place the baking tray in the preheated oven, and bake for 50 minutes.

**18.** Remove from the oven allow to cool, or serve straight away piping hot.

You can watch the full video recipe on YouTube, by scanning this QR code

**7.** Place the smaller pastry on a parchment lined baking sheet, spread a little of the cream cheese filling in the centre of the pastry, leaving a 25mm / 1in gap all around the edge. ***See image 1***

**8.** Place your frozen salmon fillet on top of the filling, and completely cover it with the remaining cream cheese filling. ***See image 2***

**9.** Brush egg wash all around the edge of the pastry right up to the filling.

**10.** Carefully place the large pastry on top, and gently press it over the filling, expelling any trapped air pockets.

**11.** Using a fork dipped in the egg wash, press all around the edge of the pastry.

**12.** Brush the whole area with the egg wash, before doing the lattice work with the thin strips of pastry as shown in the image below. ***See image 3***

| *Image: 1* | *Image: 2* | *Image: 3* |
|:---:|:---:|:---:|
| 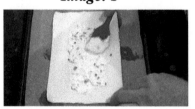 |  |  |

**13.** Give the pastry another good coat of egg wash, and get it into the preheated oven, and set your timer for 50 minutes.

**14.** Remove from the oven and allow to settle for 5 minutes on a wire rack before serving, or refrigerate, as this dish can be served hot or cold, with a nice green salad.

You can watch the full video recipe on YouTube, by scanning this QR code

# Salmon en Croute

## Ingredients

*To make the Puff pastry:*
*(See: Page 36)*

200g / 7oz skinless & boneless salmon fillet (frozen)
40g / 1½oz Mascarpone cheese
10g Chopped chives
¼ tsp / 2g Salt
¼ tsp / 1g Ground black pepper
1 Large egg and a little milk (Egg wash)

Serves Approximately 4

## Method

**1.** Chop the chives into small pieces.

**2.** Add the cream cheese to a bowl, add the salt, pepper, chives, mix until all incorporated, and set it aside.

**3.** Make up the egg wash, using the egg and milk, thoroughly whisk for 1 minute.

### *Preparing the puff pastry:*

**4.** See how to make perfect puff pastry from scratch, on **_page 36,_** it's also perfectly acceptable, to use store bought puff pastry for this recipe too.

**5.** Roll out your puff pastry to, approximately 4mm thick, you need 2 pieces, one at 23 x 18cm / 9 x 7in, and one at 23 x 15cm / 9 x 6in.
you also need 4 or 5, 13mm or ½in strips of pastry, for the lattice work.

**6.** Preheat your oven to 170°C / 340°F / Gas mark 3.

# Individual Steak pies

## Ingredients

### The Pastry:
400g / 14oz Plain or all-purpose flour
160g / mls Water
90g / 3¼oz Butter
100g / 3½oz Lard or shortening
8g / 1tsp Salt
Egg wash

### The Filling:
500g / 18oz Lean Stewing or Casserole beef.
2 Small Bay leaves (optional)
570mls / 1 Pint Beef stock
20g / 2Tbls Gravy granules

---

Makes 4 individual Pies

## Method

### Making the pastry:

1 Place the water on a low heat, and add the butter and lard to the pan, bring to a simmer.

2. Mix the salt and flour together in a bowl, and make a well in the centre.

3. Soon as the fats have melted, pour the hot liquid onto the flour well in the bowl, and bring it roughly together.

4. Tip the contents of the bowl out onto a floured worktop, and gently hand knead the pastry, until it all comes together.

5. Cut the pastry into 2 pieces, 2 thirds, for the base of the pies, and 1 third, for the tops of the pies.

6. Cover in plastic wrap or food bags, and place in the fridge for at least 1 hour before using it.

### Making the filling:

7. Dice the beef into 13mm / ½inch cubes, try not to include a lot of fat.

8. Place a medium size saucepan on a medium to high heat, and add the beef stock to slowly heat up.

9. Add the diced beef to the hot stock in the pan, and add the 2 small Bay leaves.

10. Bring it to a slow boil, turn down the heat and simmer for 1 to 1½ hours.

11. Once your meat is tender and starting to break down, remove the bay leaves.

12. Ladle out half of the stock into a jug.

13. Add the beef gravy granules to the tender meat in the saucepan, until it slightly thickens.

14. Turn off the heat, cover the pan, and allow to completely cool.

15. Grease 4 small non-stick pie tins, the dimensions of the tins I use, are 100mm x 20mm, approximately 4 x 1 inches.

16. Roll out your pastry to approx 3mm thick, and cut out 4, 12.5cm / 5in circles, for the bases of the pies, and 4, 10cm / 4in circles, for the lids of the pies.

17. Place the pastry bases in the pie tins, press the pastry right down into the corners, make sure to leave some pastry sticking over the rim of the pie tin.

You can watch the full video recipe on YouTube, by scanning this QR code

**18.** Fill the cases with the now cool beef filling, lightly compact it down, fill right to the top.

**19.** At this point, preheat your oven to, 170°C / 340°F / Gas mark 3.

**20.** Brush egg wash all around the edge of the pastry in the tin.

**21.** Brush egg wash on the underside of the lids and place the lids on the top of the pie bases, and gently press it down, using your thumbs and forefingers crimp the 2 pastries together, ***See image opposite.***

**22.** Place all 4 pies on a baking tray, and cut 2 vent slits in the top of each pie, finally give each pie a good coat of the egg wash.

**23.** Place the tray on the lowest part of the preheated oven, and use the bottom element if you have one, and bake for 40 minutes

### *Making the Gravy:*

**24.** Pour the stock from the jug we made earlier, into a small saucepan, bring to a simmer, add a couple of knobs of butter, (this will give the gravy a nice glaze)

**25.** To thicken the gravy, mix 1 tsp of cornflour/starch in 2 tbls of cold water, add it to the simmering gravy a little at a time while stirring, until you reach your required thickness.

**26.** Simmer on a very low heat for 5 minutes, with the lid on, and that is your tasty gravy done.

**27.** When the time is up, remove from the oven, place the tray on a wire rack for 5 minutes.

**28.** Carefully remove hot pies from the tins, and serve immediately, with peas and mashed potatoes or fries/chips, and lashings of that tasty gravy.

# Cheese 'n' Onion Pasty

## Ingredients

*To make the Puff pastry:*
*(See: Page 36)*

*Pasty filling:*
200g /7oz Mashed potato, No butter!
100g / 3½oz Grated Cheddar cheese
1 Small onion, finely chopped
1 Small egg, with a dash of milk, for the egg-wash
Salt & White pepper to taste

---

## Makes 4 Cheese Pasties

## Method

**1.** Mix together the mashed potato, cheese, onion and seasoning, until everything is completely combined, once mixed divide it into 4 equal pieces, do not add butter in the potatoes, it would render them too runny.

**2.** Make up the egg wash, using the egg and milk, thoroughly whisk for 1 minute.

*Preparing the puff pastry:*

**3.** *See page 36:* on how to make puff pastry from scratch, or, it is perfectly acceptable, to use store bought puff pastry for the recipe too.

**4.** Roll out your pastry into a rectangle sheet, approximately 35 x 25cm or 14 x 10in, approx 4mm thick, out of that large sheet, cut out 4 pieces, 17.5 x 12.5cm or 7 x 5in.

**5.** Place each sheet of pastry, on a slightly larger piece of floured parchment paper, stack and refrigerate them.

**6.** Take one sheet of pastry at a time, from the refrigerator, keeping it on the parchment paper.

**7.** Add some of the cheese filling to one side of the pastry, leaving a 13mm or ½in gap around the edge, *See image below.*

**8.** Brush the egg wash all around the exposed pastry, fold the pastry over the cheese filling, gently press all of the air out of it, and seal all around the edges, using the tines of a fork, this also leaves a pleasing pattern around the edges of the pasty, dip the fork tines in the egg wash, to prevent them from sticking to the pastry.

**9.** Place the pasty, whilst still on the parchment paper, onto a baking tray, repeat for the other 3 pasties, *See image opposite.*

**10.** At this point, preheat your oven to, 170°C / 340°F / Gas mark 3.

**11.** Brush each pasty liberally with the egg wash, cut 2 or 3 small vent holes in each pasty.

**12.** Place the baking tray in the preheated oven, and bake for 50 minutes.

**13.** Remove these delicious golden-brown flaky pasties from the oven, place them on a wire rack, allow them to cool and settle for 5 minutes, before serving.

You can watch the full video recipe on YouTube, by scanning this QR code

# Lemon & Vanilla Cupcake

## Ingredients

140g / 5oz Self-raising flour
140g / 5oz Caster sugar
140g / 5oz Soft salted butter
1g / ⅛tsp Bicarbonate of soda, Baking soda
2 Large eggs
22mls / 1⅛tbls Milk
6mls / 1tsp Vanilla extract

### Lemon Butter Cream:

340g / 12oz Icing / powdered sugar
170g / 6oz Soft butter
30mls / 2tbls milk
6mls / 1tsp Vanilla extract
Zest and juice of 1 medium size lemon

Makes 12 Cupcakes

## Method

### Making the cake batter:

**1.** Start by preheating your oven to 170°C / 340°F / Gas mark 3

**2.** Prepare an ordinary size 12 cup muffin tin, and line the cups with 12 standard cupcake cases.

**3.** Add the flour, Sugar, butter, and eggs to a stand mixer bowl.

**4.** Using the paddle attachment, bring the mix together on the slowest speed for a few seconds.

**5.** Once it has all combined, speed up the machine to medium fast, and mix for exactly 1 minute.

**6.** Stop the machine, and reset your timer to 30 seconds, and add the milk and vanilla.

**7.** Restart the machine on medium fast again for 30 seconds this time.

**8.** Evenly divide the cake batter, between the 12 cake cases.

**9.** Place the muffin tray in the preheated oven, and set the timer for 20 minutes.

**10.** Once the time is up, place the muffin tray on a wire rack, Leave them there, until the cakes are completely cooled.

### *Making the Lemon butter cream frosting:*

**11.** Add all of the butter cream ingredients to a bowl, and blend them all together, using a spatula.

**12.** Once the mixture is combined, whip it for one minute, using a balloon hand whisk.

**13.** Add a few drops of yellow food colouring, and whisk again for a few seconds, until the colour is even.

**14.** Once your frosting is ready, spoon it into a piping bag, with a medium size star nozzle attached.

**15.** When your cakes have completely cooled, pipe the butter cream onto the cake, try to do this in one movement.

**16.** Add whatever decoration you like, sprinkles etc.

You can watch the full video recipe on YouTube, by scanning this QR code

# Lemon Drizzle Sandwich Cake

## Ingredients

**T*he Sponge:***
200g / 7½ oz softened salted Butter
200g / 7½ oz Caster Sugar
250g / 9 oz Self Raising Flour ( if you use all-Purpose or Plain flour, add an extra 2 tsps of baking powder to the recipe)
4 Large Eggs
8g / 2tsp Baking Powder
6mls / 1tsp of Lemon or Vanilla Extract
Zest of 1 lemon

**The Filling:**
300mls of double or Heavy Cream
10g / 2tsp Icing or Powdered Sugar
1tsp Vanilla Extract
100g / 3½oz Lemon curd

**The Drizzle:**
Zest and juice of 1 lemon
45g / 3tbles Granulated sugar

Approximately 6 slices

## Method

### Making the sponge:

**1.** Begin the recipe by preheating your oven to 190°C / 374°F / Gas mark 5.

**2.** Grease two 20cm / 8in sandwich cake tins, and line the bottoms with greaseproof paper.

**3.** Add the butter and caster sugar to a bowl, using a spatula, cream them together, to a smooth paste, the mix in the zest and extract.

**4.** Whisk in the eggs, 1 at a time (make sure your eggs are at room temperature).

**5.** Sift in the flour and baking powder, and gently fold it into the batter, using a spatula.

**6.** Divide the batter equally into the 2 cake tins, level the batter off, give the tins a light tap on the bench, and get them into the preheated oven, and set your timer for 25 minutes.

### Making the filling, and the lemon drizzle:

**7. *The Cream:*** While the cakes are baking, start making the chantilly cream, and the lemon drizzle topping

**8.** Add the double, or heavy whipping cream, vanilla extract, and icing sugar, to a bowl, and whisk until thick, and has stiff peaks, refrigerate until needed.

**9. *The Drizzle:*** Zest and juice the 1 medium size lemon, to a small bowl, add the granulated sugar and zest of the lemon, now add 2 tablespoons of the lemon juice, mix until thick, but runny, set it aside for now.

**10.** After the time is up, check that the sponges are done  (don't open the oven door beforehand) use a cocktail stick to test that the cake is done, if it comes out clean, the cake has finished baking, if not give it a couple of more minutes.

**11.** Place the tins on a wire rack for 10 minutes, after the 10 minutes, carefully remove the sponges from the tins, and gently peel off the parchment paper, allow the cakes to completely cool for a further 10 minutes.

**12.** Once cooled, place one of the sponges on a serving plate, with the bottom of the sponge cake facing up.

**13.** Cover the surface of the cake with a good helping of the lemon curd, but staying approximately 5mm shy of the edge.

**14.** Next, cover the lemon curd with a thick layer of the chantilly cream that was made earlier.

**15.** Now very gently, line up and place the second sponge cake on top of the cream, with the flat bottom of the sponge facing down this time, gently press it down.

**16.** Finally, brush or pour over the lemon drizzle mixture, allowing it to cascade over the edge of the cake, for aesthetic reasons, try to control the spacing and direction the drizzles, using your pastry brush.

You can watch the full video recipe on YouTube, by scanning this QR code

# Easy Chocolate Cake

## Ingredients

175g / 6½oz Self Raising Flour
*( if you use all-Purpose or Plain flour, add an extra 2 tsps of baking powder to the recipe)*
175g / 6½oz Vegetable oil
4 Large eggs
90g / 3oz Granulated sugar
30g / 1oz Golden syrup or Corn syrup
30g / 1oz Cocoa powder
1tsp Baking powder
1tsp Vanilla extract
½tsp Salt
100g / 3½oz chocolate hazelnut spread

---

Serves Approximately 6

---

## Method

**1.** Start the recipe by greasing and flouring a 900g / 2lb loaf tin, the loaf tin dimensions are 23 x 12 x 7cm / 9 x 5 x 3in

**2.** Preheat your oven to 170°C / 338°F / Gas mark 4

**3.** to a large bowl, add the 4 eggs, sugar, the golden or corn syrup, oil, and the vanilla extract, give it a good whisk for 1 minute.

**4.** Sift in the all of the dry ingredients, that's the flour, cocoa powder, and the baking powder, gently fold those in, using a whisk or a spatula, you should now have a silky smooth, but a fairly runny batter.

**5.** Carefully pour the batter into the prepared loaf tin.

**6.** Give the tin a couple of taps on the worktop, this will lift any of the larger air bubbles.

**7.** Now get it into the preheated oven, and set your timer for 50 minutes.

You can watch the full video recipe on YouTube, by scanning this QR code

**8.** When the time's up, check it with a cocktail stick, if it comes out clean, the cake's done, if not give it another 5 minutes, once done take the cake out of the oven, and let it rest, still in the tin, and on a wire rack for 5 minutes.

**9.** Carefully remove the cake from the tin, and let it sit on the wire rack for 15 minutes.

**10.** Once it is relatively cool, cover the top with the Hazelnut chocolate spread, slice and serve with a nice cup of coffee or tea.

# Blueberry Muffins

## Ingredients

400g / 14oz Self Raising Flour
(*if you use all-Purpose or Plain flour,
add an extra 2 tsps of baking powder
to the recipe*)
250g / 9oz Unsalted butter (cubed)
2 Large eggs (beaten)
120mls Full fat milk
170g / 6oz Castor sugar
1tsp Baking powder
1tsp Vanilla extract
4g / ½tsp Salt
300g / 11oz Blueberries

### Makes 12 Muffins

## Method

**1.** Start by preheating your oven to 180°C / 355°F / Gas mark 4

**2.** Prepare an ordinary size 12 cup muffin tin, line the cups with 12 standard size muffin paper cases.

**3.** Add the cubed butter to a large mixing bowl, sift in, the flour, baking powder, and salt, rub these ingredients together with your fingers until your mix resembles fine bread crumbs.

**4.** Add the sugar, and mix it in.

**5.** Time to add the wet ingredients, pour in the milk, eggs, and vanilla extract, using a spatula, blend all the ingredients together, until you have a smooth fairly stiff batter.

**6.** Do not add the blueberries to the mixture at this point, they would only break up, and turn your batter blue, they need to be added later.

**7.** Using a teaspoon, add a little of the mixture to the bottom of each muffin case, and place 2 or 3 blueberries on top of the mixture, add another full teaspoon of the mixture, on top of the blueberries, repeat this procedure, until the muffin cases are filled to the top.

**8.** Once all of your muffins have been built up, get the muffin tray into the preheated oven, and set your timer for 25 minutes.

**9.** When the time is up, place the muffin tray on a wire rack for 5 minutes, allowing the muffins to settle a while.

**10.** After the five minutes, take the out of the muffin tray and place the cases onto the wire rack, and allow them to completely cool before having them, with a nice cup of coffee of tea.

You can watch the full video recipe on YouTube, by scanning this QR code

# Fresh Cream Gateau

## Ingredients

**The sponge:**
112g / 4oz Selfraising flour
( if you use all-Purpose or Plain flour,
add an extra 4g / 1tsp of baking
powder to the recipe)
4 large eggs: yolks separated
112g / 4oz Sugar
30g / 2tbls Milk
30g / 2tbls Vegetable oil
2g / ¼tsp Salt
6g / 1tsp Vanilla extract

**The filling:**
300g / mls Double / whipping /
heavy cream
150g / 5½oz Jam of your choice
6g / 1tsp Vanilla extract
12g / ½oz Icing / powdered sugar

---

Approximately 6 slices

---

## Method

**Making the sponge cake:**

**1.** Line a 18 x 8cm / 7 x 3in baking tin, with parchment paper, sides and bottom.

**2.** Separate the egg yolks from the white, and divide the 112g of sugar into 3 equal parts, approx 37.5g each.

**3.** Add the egg whites to a stand mixer, and using the whisk attachment, start whisking on medium to high speed, adding the 3 parts of sugar, at 1 minute intervals, your final meringue should have stiff pointy peaks.

**4.** Add the vanilla extract to the egg yolks, and whisk by hand for 1 minute, until foamy, and light in colour, add the egg yolk mixture to the meringue, and whisk for 30 seconds, until it is all amalgamated.

**5.** At this point, it's time to preheat your oven to, 170°C that's 340°F or Gas mark 3.

**6.** Next remove the bowl from the machine, and sift in the flour and the salt, I'm using self-raising flour in this recipe, which already contains baking powder, but if you are using plain, or all-purpose flour, you'll need to add 1tsp that's, 4g of baking powder.

**7.** Using a spatula, gently fold the flour into the mixture, don't over mix, or you will knock the air out of the mixture.

**8.** Put your oil and milk into a small bowl, and add 2 tbls of your cake batter, and whisk them together, then gently fold this mixture, back into your cake batter.

**9.** Carefully pour your cake batter into the prepared baking tin, place in the middle of your pre-heated oven, and set your timer for 40 minutes.

**Making the Chantilly cream:**

**10.** Add the cream, vanilla extract, and the sugar, into a bowl, and whisk until the cream thickens to stiff peaks, cover and refrigerate, using an electric hand mixer, this should take around 3 to 4 minutes, ( FYI, this can be made hours in advance)

You can watch the full video recipe on YouTube, by scanning this QR code

**11.** When the time is up, remove the cake from the oven, and immediately turn it out of the tin, place it on a wire rack for 30 minutes, before removing the paper.

**12.** Cut the cake into 3 layers, (see video for tips on how to uniformly cut the cake, scan the QR code opposite).

**13.** Place the bottom sponge layer on a serving plate, or cake stand, and add a thin coat of a jam of your choice, then add a layer of your Chantilly cream on top of the jam, add the middle cake layer, and repeat the filling of jam and cream.

**14.** Place the last sponge on the top, gently compressing it, and give the top a good sprinkle of Icing/powdered sugar, to finish it off.

**15.** Place the cake in the refrigerator for an hour to allow the jam and cream to stiffen up before slicing and serving, serve with a nice cup of coffee or tea.

# Scotch Eggs

## Ingredients

6 Medium size eggs (boiled)
500g / 18oz Pork or beef
Sausage meat
2 Large eggs, (Beaten)
200g / 7oz Bread crumbs
2g / ½tsp Dried Sage
1g / ¼tsp White pepper
Oil for frying

_____

### Makes 6 Scotch eggs

## Method

**1.** Start the recipe by boiling the eggs, 8 minutes for hard boiled egg, 6 minutes for soft boiled eggs, once boiled place them in cold water, this will stop them cooking anymore, (always use eggs straight from the fridge for this recipe)

**2.** Buy or make 200g / 7oz of bread crumbs, and beat the 2 large eggs.

**3.** Add the pepper and sage to your sausage meat, and mix well, then divide the meat into 6 x 83g / 3oz portions.

**4.** Crack and peel the now cold boiled eggs.

**5.** Place a small piece of cling film on your worktop (approx. 20cm / 8in square) and grease with a little oil.

**6.** Place a portion of the sausage meat on the cling film, and flatten it out into a 13 x 8cm / 5 x 3in rectangle with your fingers.

**7.** Place a boiled egg in the middle of the meat, *See image opposite:* and pick it all up, using the cling film, place it in the palm of your hand, and form the meat around the egg, nipping and pressing the meat edges together, until the egg is completely covered, once the egg has been formed, remove the cling film, tidy it up and set it aside, carry on forming the rest of the scotch eggs.

**8.** To coat the eggs, dip each one in the beaten egg, and make sure it is well coated, then add it to the bread crumbs until it is completely covered, for a crispier coating, repeat these 2 stages again, continue until all 6 scotch eggs are made.

**9.** In a deep medium size pan, heat up the oil to approximately 130 to 135°C that's 265 to 275°F

**10.** Very carefully! lower each scotch egg into the hot oil, one at a time, using a slotted spoon, you can fry 3 or 4 at the same time, fry for 6 to 7 minutes until golden brown.

**11.** Remove from the pan and drain on kitchen paper, can be served hot or cold, I have mine hot, with a mixed salad, chips/fries, and salad cream, also ideal for adult or children's lunch boxes, or picnics.

You can watch the full video recipe on YouTube, by scanning this QR code

**12.** For a healthier option to frying, these delicious scotch eggs can be baked too, preheat your oven 10 minutes before baking, to 200°C / 390°F or Gas mark 6.

**13.** Spray all the scotch eggs with a low calorie cooking oil, place all 6 scotch eggs on a parchment lined baking tray, once your oven is at temperature, bake in the middle of the oven for 30 minutes.

**14.** *Scan the QR code right, to see the baked version video*

*Scan this QR code: to see the video for the healthier baked version of these scotch eggs*

# Beef Stew
# &
# Crispy Dumplings

## Ingredients

### The Beef stew:

1kg / 2lb.3oz Casserole or stewing Beef
570mls / 1 pint Beef Stock
570mls / 1 pint Strong Beer or Stout
2 Large Carrots
1 small turnip or swede
1 Large Leek
1 Large Onion
4 Cloves of Garlic
½tsp Dried Thyme
½tsp Freshly Ground Pepper
4g / ½tsp Salt
100g / 3½oz Plain Flour / All Purpose Flour
30mls /2tbls of cooking oil
2 heaped tsp of Corn flour/starch
in 150mls of cold water (thickener)
2 bay leaves (optional)

### The crispy Dumplings:

300g / 10½oz Self- Raising Flour
2tsp Baking Powder
175mls of full fat milk
60g / 2oz of butter
100g / 3½oz Beef or vegetable suet
1 Large Egg
100g / 3½oz Finely Chopped Leek

## Serves Approximately 6

## Method

**1.** Start by preparing the dumplings.

**2.** Finely chop the leeks from the dumpling ingredients list.

**3.** In a large bowl, sift in the SR flour, and baking powder, *( if you use all-Purpose or Plain flour, add an extra 2 tsps of baking powder to the recipe)*

**4.** Rub the cold butter into the flour, using your fingers, until it resembles fine bread crumbs.

**5.** Add the finely chopped leeks, and the beef or vegetable suet, lightly and gently, toss all the ingredients together, using your fingers, until thoroughly mixed.

**6.** If you can't find suet, add an extra 100g / 3½oz of cold butter to the previous rubbing in step.

**7.** Whisk the egg and milk together, and add it to the bowl, with an ordinary dinner knife, cut the mixture together, until it becomes a sticky mass.

**8.** Cover the bowl with a dry clean towel, and let it relax at room temperature until needed.

*5-Quart: Cast Iron Dutch Oven*

### Making the beef stew:

**9.** You'll need a large casserole dish or pan to make this, I like to use my 5 quart cast iron Dutch oven.

**10.** Cut your beef into large chunks, coat and toss them in the flour and set them aside for now.

**11.** Wash, peel and chop your carrots, turnip, leeks, and onion into large pieces.

**12.** Peel and finely chop your garlic cloves.

**13.** Brown off your floured beef chunks, in a large frying pan, do this in 2 or 3 batches, once all the beef is browned off, transfer them to a dish, and deglaze the frying pan with a little of the beef stock from the recipe, then pour it back into your stock pot.

**14.** Preheat your oven to 160°C / 320°F / Gas mark 3.

**15.** Time to assemble, on a medium heat, under your Dutch oven, or large pan, add all of the chopped vegetables, then add your browned beef, and mix them all together.

**16.** Add your garlic, herbs, salt and pepper, then add your beer, followed by the beef stock, and bring it to a light boil.

**17.** Once it reaches boiling point, get the lid on the pot, and get it into the preheated oven, set your timer for 2 hours.

**18.** Mix up the corn flour/starch with the cold water and set it aside, this is your thickening agent.

**19.** After the 2 hours carefully take the stew pot out of the oven, and onto a low hob ring, give your thickener a final stir, and pour it in the stew whilst stirring until it thickens.

**20.** Using a dessert spoon, add the dumpling mixture to the beef stew, equally spacing them out (remember these dumplings will double in size as they cook) to prevent the mixture sticking to the spoon, dip it in the gravy every time.

**21.** Without the lid on this time, place the pot back in the oven, and increase the temperature to 180°C / 355°F or gas mark 5, set you timer for 30 minutes.

**22.** Serve piping hot straight from the oven.

You can watch the full video recipe on YouTube, by scanning this QR code